Instruments
of the
Craft

**Mastering the Four Tools
of the Witch**

T0405506

About the Author

Raven Grimassi (1951-2019) was a prolific occult author who had written more than twenty books on various magical, pagan, and occult topics. He is best known for his work in popularizing the branch of Italian witchcraft known as Stregheria and was an active member of the pagan community for decades. He died March 10, 2019 and is survived by not only his books, but also his loving wife Stephanie who continues to make magic in his name.

Instruments
of the
Craft

**MASTERING THE FOUR TOOLS
OF THE WITCH**

Raven Grimassi

Chicago, Illinois

Paperback ISBN: 978-1-964537-11-5
Library of Congress Control Number on file.

Disclaimer: Crossed Crow Books, LLC does not participate in, endorse, or have any authority or responsibility concerning private business transactions between our authors and the public. Any internet references contained in this work were found to be valid during the time of publication, however, the publisher cannot guarantee that a specific reference will continue to be maintained. This book's material is not intended to diagnose, treat, cure, or prevent any disease, disorder, ailment, or any physical or psychological condition. The author, publisher, and its associates shall not be held liable for the reader's choices when approaching this book's material. The views and opinions expressed within this book are those of the author alone and do not necessarily reflect the views and opinions of the publisher.

Published by:
Crossed Crow Books, LLC
518 Davis St., Suite 205
Evanston, IL 60201
www.crossedcrowbooks.com

Printed in the United States of America.
IBI

More Books from Raven Grimassi

Witchcraft: A Mystery Tradition

*Crafting a Tradition of Witchcraft: Building a
Foundation for Your Magical Beliefs & Practices*

*Cauldron of Memory: Retrieving Ancestral
Knowledge and Wisdom*

*Raven's Call: A Quaint and Curious Anthology
of Forgotten Lore*

*A Grimoire of Italian Witchcraft: Practical Spells
& Rituals of the Old Religion*

*The Witches' Craft: The Roots of Witchcraft
& Magical Transformation*

Wiccan Magick: Inner Teachings of the Craft

Wiccan Mysteries: Ancient Origins & Teachings

Contents

Introduction

Instruments of the Craft, in essence, offers an in-depth study of the four classical tools of the Witch known as the pentacle, wand, athame, and chalice. It consists of six chapters:

- **Chapter One** covers teachings related to the creative Elements of Earth, Air, Fire, and Water. Each Element's nature and role in magick and ritual is thoroughly examined. This chapter also explores the directional quarters of the ritual circle: North, East, South, and West.

- **Chapter Two** explores the pentacle as a tool that draws upon the creative Element of Earth, its use on the altar, and its role at the four quarters (North, East, South, and West). The chapter also includes a method of preparing and charging the tool.

- **Chapter Three** examines the wand as a tool that draws upon the Element of Air or Fire (this differs between traditions). Additionally, the chapter explores the wand's use in evocation and invocation and provides a method of preparing and charging the tool.

- **Chapter Four** explores the ritual knife known as the *athame*, which is connected to the Element of Fire or Air (this differs between traditions). The athame is a tool of transformation and is often used to cast a ritual or magickal circle. This chapter explores the use of the athame and provides a method of preparing and charging the tool.

- **Chapter Five** examines the chalice (or ritual cup) as a tool associated with the Element of Water. It explores the chalice as a spiritual tool and a ceremonial vessel and, like the other chapters, includes a method of preparing and charging the tool.

- **Chapter Six** explores the circle as a "place between the worlds," exploring its mystical and practical aspects. Additionally, the chapter discusses the ritual circle's relationship to the "Elemental Portals" into the Spirit Realm and to the Guardians of the cardinal points: North, East, South, and West. The chapter concludes with a magickal circle casting ritual.

At the end of each chapter, you will have an opportunity to test your knowledge. In Appendix A, you will find answers to the questions. If you struggle with the test, reread the chapter at a slower pace and try again.

Chapter I:

The Four Creative Elements

In the world of magick and ritual, we find teachings regarding four creative Elements: Earth, Air, Fire, and Water. They are used for various purposes in the art of ritual and magick, most commonly to create a ritual or magickal space known as the Circle of the Arts (in which practitioners gather to perform magick or ritual). Additionally, the Four Elements can empower spells and other works of magick. The idea of the Four Elements is rooted in the concept that everything on the physical plane has a non-material counterpart. This concept belongs to the field of metaphysics, which is a philosophy concerned with the fundamental nature of reality and being. According to metaphysical philosophy, the four "building blocks" of creation existed before anything of a material nature. One of the oldest writings on this subject comes from ancient Greek myths. The ancient Greek philosopher Empedocles is credited with revealing a cohesive understanding of the Four Elements. One example is his work titled *The Doctrine of the Four Elements* or the *Tetrasomia*. The early creation myths depict the Universe in chaos. Only the Elemental Forces of Earth, Air, Fire, and Water occupied the great void. Each of the Elements was separate and independent. They did not work together, and there was no purpose or direction. All was in disorder. Because of this condition, creation was not possible.

In the midst of chaos, the Fifth Element of Spirit appeared.[1] Ancient text refers to it as *aether,* often thought of as the Divine Mind. The Fifth Element drew the forces of Earth, Air, Fire, and Water together into harmony. Each became an integral tool for creation and, once the Elements were unified, the worlds were created.

---

1   Aristotle. *On the Heavens.* Translated by J.L. Stocks, *The Internet Classics Archive,* MIT, classics.mit.edu/Aristotle/heavens.html.

In a similar style, the Four Elements are used to create a mini-universe that emerges from "casting a circle" for ritual or magickal purposes. In effect, you become the Fifth Element and bring the Elemental Forces together in unison. These forces give form and vitality to the created space. They also mark out the boundaries of the circle as a place set apart from the everyday world. The lesson in Chapter Six examines this in detail.

The following material is important to understand the Four Elements and how they empower ritual tools. Don't allow yourself to be overwhelmed by the material but just read through it and do your best to understand. Future chapters will bring everything into place, so, for now, just read and get as much as possible out of the lesson.

The Elemental Square

The relation between the Powers and the Elements is represented in the well-known Elemental Square or Square of Opposition. The square places the Four Elements into the qualities assigned to them in occult correspondences and sets them in relationship to one another. Through this, we can study their occult natures and better understand how to work with them. The following concepts are tricky to understand at first, so do not dwell on them too much at this point. If confused, reread the chapter to have an overall better understanding. You will be acclimated with the concepts, and it will feel more familiar with another readthrough.

The illustration on page 7 shows the general layout of the Elements and their correspondences.

The Elemental Square describes Earth as dry and cool, Water as cool and moist, Air as moist and warm, and Fire as warm and dry.

Each Element possesses one force that is dominant. Earth is predominantly dry, Water predominantly cool, Air predominantly moist, and Fire predominantly warm. The dominant force for each Element is the one situated counterclockwise from it in the Elemental Square of Opposition direction, with arrows indicating the direction toward each Element's dominant power.

In the illustration, the vertical dotted line represents the active qualities (warm, cool) while the horizontal dotted line represents the passive qualities (moist, dry). The upper Elements (Air, Fire) are active, light, and ascending. The lower Elements (Water, Earth) are passive, heavy, and descending. The Elements on the right are pure, extreme, and absolute light (Fire) or heavy (Earth). Those on the left are mixed, intermediate, and relatively light (Air) or heavy (Water). The Organic Cycle (the cycle of the seasons) goes sunwise around the square.

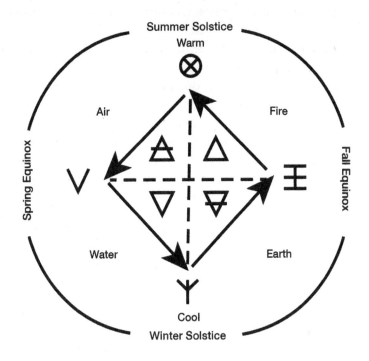

Unlike the material chemical elements, the mystical spiritual Elements can be transformed into each other by applying the laws discovered by Aristotle. Understanding these laws is a prerequisite to transform and combine them in their various manifestations. In essence, one Element can be transformed directly into another only if they share a common quality (and are thus adjacent, not opposed, on the Elemental Square). For example, Water is transformed into Air when it is acted on by a larger quantity of Air, since the Water's coolness is "overpowered" by the Air's warmth; the common moist quality is retained through the transformation. This process is reversible, since Air can be transformed back into Water by acting upon it with sufficient Water.

Direct transformation between opposing Elements is impossible. Water cannot be transformed directly into Fire, since they have no common quality to give continuity to the process. However, Water can be transformed indirectly by changing it first into Air or Earth. This occurs when the Water is acted upon by a larger quantity of Fire. We can move around the Square, but not across it.

The Pentagram Symbolism

The popular image of the five-pointed star within a circle represents the power of the Four Elements. In its position with one tip upward, the star represents "Spirit" over matter—the Four Elements united in a "common cause" by the Divine. In this light, the presence of the pentagram signifies that the

ability to manifest or dissolve is in the hands of the person holding or wearing the pentagram. It puts spirits and entities on notice that they are subject to the combined power of the Four Elements and Divinity, which can be wielded by the practitioner or ritualist.

The pentagram shows the Four Elements in a different order than they appear on the Elemental Square. This arrangement comes from occult orders like the Golden Dawn and is designed to evoke the Elemental Forces. In contrast, the Elemental Square is designed to show the relationship between the Four Elements.

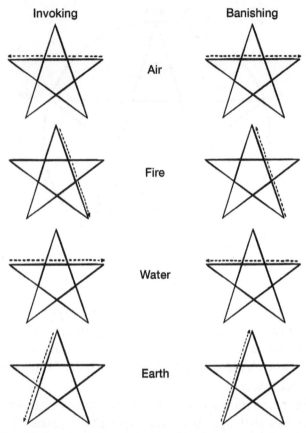

The illustration above shows the placement of each Elemental Nature on the five-pointed star. At the top of the star appears the symbol of Spirit or Divinity, which is the directing force that makes the Elemental Forces accessible to the ritualist. The pentagram's symbolism signifies that the user invokes the higher selfless nature of Spirit when performing magick, rather than being driven by selfish motives.

Access to the Four Elements and the ability to command them lets the user collect and direct their creative nature, empowering rituals and works of magick. A popular method of evoking and releasing Elemental Forces (often called banishing) calls for tracing the star in the air with a ritual tool. To evoke, the star is traced towards the desired Element. To release, the star is traced away from the Element. In all cases, the entire star is traced back to the point of origin.

The Element of Earth

In magick, Earth is the cohesive and condensing force. It is the anchor of manifestation. The Element of Earth provides and maintains the stability required to take form and manifest in the Material Plane. In the art of magick, the Elemental Earth is associated with the tool known as the pentacle. This is covered in the lesson in Chapter Two.

In modern times, some systems assign the color green to the Earth as a ritual and magickal correspondence. In other magickal systems, the Earth is yellow, connecting it to the Sun that causes the soil to birth plants. In other words, yellow is the vital essence that awakens fertility in the Earth. Most systems assign the Element of Earth to the North in a ritual or magickal circle.

Each Element has a "tonal" assigned that aids in its activation. The tonal for Earth is the English letter "a" and, when spoken, it is stretched out and carried upon the utterance: *A-a-a-a-a*.

The Element of Air

In magickal terms, Air is the transmissional Elemental Force. As a Force, it carries or conveys. This connects Elemental Air with communication. Magickally, Air is often used to pass a magickal intention into something. This is a form of "charging" an object through magick.

In ritual, the Elemental Air is associated with the tool known as the wand or the athame. This differs from tradition to tradition. In the case of the athame, the association is that the blade cuts through the air. In the case of the wand, the association is that the wand was once a branch moved by the air.

In modern times, most systems assign the color yellow to Air as a ritual and magickal correspondence. This is associated with the idea of the Sun in the sky. The older tradition assign blue to Air (because the sky looks blue in daylight). Most systems assign the Element of Air to the East in a ritual or magickal circle.

The tonal for Air is the English letter "e" and is stretched out and carried upon the utterance: *E-e-e-e-e*.

The Element of Fire

Fire is the Element of transformation. Whatever Fires touches, it changes. Set fire to paper, and the result is ash. In this regard, fire can create, and it can destroy. Fire forges metal in a tool and likewise melts one into liquid.

In modern times, most systems assign the color red to Fire as a ritual and magickal correspondence. This is because fire makes things red hot. Most systems assign the Element of Fire to the South in a ritual or magickal circle.

The tonal for Fire is the English letter "i" and is stretched out and carried upon the utterance: *I-i-i-i-i*.

The Element of Water

Water is the Element of motion or movement. It is also a purifying and dissolving Element and, in this sense, removes the previous state of being.

In modern times, most systems assign the color blue to Water as a ritual and magickal correspondence. This is associated with the color of the sky reflected on the surface of the water, which makes the water look blue. The older assignment is the color green, which is how stormy water appears, thus depicting its power. Most systems assign the Element of Water to the West in a ritual or magickal circle.

The tonal for Water is the English letter "o" and is stretched out and carried upon the utterance: *O-o-o-o-o*.

The Elemental Plane

In metaphysical teachings, there are seven planes of existence that comprise the Universe. These are called the Unknowable, Divine, Spiritual, Mental, Astral, Elemental, and Material. The Elemental Plane is also known as the Plane of Forces, and it contains the energies that we call Earth, Air, Fire, and Water.

The Elemental Plane is directly connected to the Physical Plane and serves to empower, nourish, and animate the material world. One way to think of it is as a current of energy flowing through the Earth into the Astral Dimension and then returning to complete the circuit. In this river of Elemental energy, the thoughts and desires emanating from the Physical Dimension are carried. In effect, the Elemental current delivers them to the astral level, which in turn shapes what they symbolize into animated images. The energy of these astral forms is then carried back to the Physical Dimension by the flow of Elemental energy into the material world.

The Elemental Plane connects to the Physical Plane, and, through it, Elemental activity helps renew the vitality within nature. In ancient myths, we find many accounts in which humans and nature spirits come into contact and form various relationships. The ancient teachings tell us that the veil between the worlds was thinner because humans had not yet developed enough to negatively impact nature. Therefore, the vibrations within the natural world were more attuned to the Elemental Realms. With newer technologies, the developments in the Iron Age gave our ancestors more tools that changed and impacted our reliance and relationship with nature.

Like other metals, iron is an effective magnet because its electrons do not oppose each other's spin. Therefore, each iron atom is in effect a tiny magnet. Magnets tend to align the atoms of other metals, making them magnets as well. A magnet produces a field that affects other electro-magnetic fields. Elemental beings have a polarity of their own, which allows them to cross between the Physical Plane and their own dimension. Iron is very disturbing to the energy fields of these beings and they have a natural aversion to it. In myth and legends, fairies have a fear of iron, and it is used against them in folklore. Lodestones (natural magnets) and iron amulets have been used to ward fairies and defend against magick in general.

Nature of the Elements

Just as there is polarity in some occult concepts, the Elements have "negative" aspects. In this context, we may say that Earth is rigid, Air is flighty, Fire is destructive, and Water is stagnant. The Four Elements are kept in a positive and peaceful state through the mediation of Spirit, which can be called the Fifth Element. It is important to understand that when we speak of the Four Elements, we refer to types of energy. The physical forms of the Four Elements are manifestations of Elemental principles and not the material elements themselves.

As mentioned earlier, Empedocles (a student of the teachings of Pythagoras) was the first person known to have taught the concept of the Four Elements as a single cohesive doctrine. He was also the first to introduce the Four Elements into astrology to describe the basic nature of zodiac signs.

These are the traditional assignments in some European occult systems, which are derived from the teachings of Empedocles:

Earth: Taurus, Virgo, Capricorn
Air: Gemini, Libra, Aquarius
Fire: Aries, Leo, Sagittarius
Water: Cancer, Scorpio, Pisces

Earth: Cold and dry
Air: Hot and moist
Fire: Hot and dry
Water: Cold and moist

In Roman mythology, the four winds are deities with Elemental natures. Their names are Boreas [*bor-ee-us*], Eurus [*your-us*], Notus [*no-tuss*], and Zephyrus [*zeh-for-us*]. Boreas is associated with the North, Eurus with the East, Notus with the South, and Zephyrus with the West. They are controlled by another deity named Aeolus [*Ay-oh-lus*] who was the guardian of the winds, keeping them in order by chaining them together.² In this myth, we see the Four Elements controlled by a fifth non-elemental power. This, of course, is the basic symbolism of the pentagram. It is interesting to note that Pythagoras and his disciples considered the five-pointed star a sacred symbol. In the fifth century BCE, the followers of Pythagoras revered the pentagram,³ which was later adopted into Freemasonry and Wicca.

Some Occultists credit Philippus Aureolus Paracelsus with what can be called the "Doctrine of the Four Elements." Paracelsus was a sixteenth century alchemist who taught that the four primary Elements consist of both a vaporous and a tangible substance. He believed that each Element existed as both a physical element and a spiritual Element. Paracelsus taught that just as there were two types of matter in nature, a physical and etheric, so too must there be two types of nature (the Physical World and the Supernatural World). He further believed that within the Supernatural World there existed beings native to each of the Elemental Regions therein.

---

2   Virgil, *The Aeneid,* Translated by Robert Fagles (Penguin Classics, 2006) Book 1, lines 52-55.

3   Burkert, Walter, *Lore and Science in Ancient Pythagoreanism* (Harvard University Press, 1972) 468.

Thus, Paracelsus assigned gnomes to Earth, sylphs to Air, salamanders to Fire, and undines to Water.

During the Middle Ages in Christian Europe, people believed to have composite natures, meaning that they had both a spiritual and physical existence. Elemental beings were considered creatures of a single nature related entirely to the property of their corresponding Element. Just as fish are creatures of the water and birds are creatures of the air, each Elemental is unique in form and function in a way that is appropriate to its Elemental environment. Paracelsus taught that Elementals were invisible to human sight because they existed in a more subtle state than physical forms or phenomena. It was believed, however, that by condensing the etheric material of their forms, Elementals could appear in the physical world of nature whenever they pleased. As Paracelsus stated, the Elementals live in the interior Elements while men and women live in the exterior elements.[4]

The Elementals
Gnomes
Gnomes are beings who inhabit the etheric Elemental material of the Earth's Spiritual Dimension. They possess a vibratory rate that makes them invisible to humans, but one that is still close enough to the lower physical vibration for them to interact. Their actions are reflected in the presence

---

4   Paracelsus, *Liber de Nymphis, Sylphis, Pygmaeis et Salamandris et de Caeteris Spiritibus,* Translated in *The Hermetic and Alchemical Writings of Paracelsus,* edited by Arthur Edward Waite, Vol. 1 (James Elliott and Co., 1894) 216.

of mineral deposits, the erosion of rock, and the formation of crystals and other geological formations.

In some occult philosophies, the gnomes were protectors of secret treasures concealed beneath the Earth in vast caverns. In the past, some people taught that gnomes were not naturally inclined to aid humankind. However, if a person won their confidence and trust, they would prove to be valuable allies. Like all Elementals, it was dangerous to deceive them or misuse their aid. Elementals work through the subjective nature of people and can influence the human mind, bringing gloom, melancholy, and despair. Conversely, they can bestow confidence, steadfastness, and endurance.

In occult circles, the gnomes are ruled by a king whose name is Gob. They usually appear to humans as small dwarf-like creatures.

Sylphs

Sylphs live in the etheric Elemental substance of Air, which is the spiritual medium of our atmosphere. Their activity is reflected in the gathering of clouds, the formation of snow-flakes, and the growth and maturity of all plant life. In the past, they were called the spirits of the wind and were the source of many Greek myths and legends. Among the Elementals as a whole, sylphs are of the highest vibration and can thus traverse the dimensions at will.

The sylphs have a ruler whose name is Paralda. Though essentially creatures of the air, Sylphs reside upon high mountain tops. Legend has it that they once spoke to humans through caverns and were the voices of ancient oracles.

Sylphs are associated with the activity of the human mind. They can influence and inspire humans. They are often said to gather around the poet or artist to impart their inner visions of spiritual beauty. They usually appear to humans in the classic fairy image.

Salamanders

Salamanders live in the etheric Elemental substance of nature's fire. It is through their activity that fire exists and can be used by humankind. Some believe that Fire elementals were the first to befriend humans, teaching our ancestors how to make campfires. Lore tells us that salamanders are ruled by a king called Djin.

Salamanders move about most freely at night, appearing as balls of light drifting across various bodies of water.

Salamanders have a profound effect upon human nature since they are linked to the activity of our bodies through which we maintain a body temperature. They influence our emotions and general temperament. When we say that someone is "hot-blooded" or "hot-headed," we are referring to their Elemental nature. Salamanders often appear to humans in the shape of small lizard-like flames.

Undines

Undines live in the etheric Elemental substance of humidity and within liquids. They are recalled in the images of water nymphs and mermaids. Springs, streams, and wells are favored by undines. Their traditional abodes were among marsh reeds and vegetation growing alongside rivers and lakes.

The undines are ruled by Necksa. They are friendly towards humans and their presence has a strong influence upon our emotional well-being. The moodiness of an individual can be traced to their Elemental nature. Just as water can be beautiful in a fall or river, it can also be unattractive in a stagnant pond. When we say a person is "washed-out," we are speaking of an Elemental influence.

The activity of undines is responsible for the vitality within all liquids and therefore plays a vital role in plant, animal, and human life. Undines appear to humans most often in full human shape. Some occultists believe the beautiful maidens associated with lakes and waterfalls in mythology were Undines.

The Elements and Consciousness

Elemental energies can be drawn into the physical body and human consciousness for magickal purposes. One reason for doing this is to create a balance of Elemental natures within the psyche. According to some occult beliefs, positive and negative personality traits are attributed to Elemental conditions within the aura. The personality of the individual can be balanced by bringing the Elements into a proportional harmony. Traits related to vigor and vitality are associated with Fire. Those related to strength and endurance are connected to Earth. Traits associated with adaptability are linked to Water. Those of Air are related to creativity.

An imbalance of Elemental energies can result in one Element dominating another or lead to the opposite qualities of an Element emerging. For example, a "hyper-nature" can have an overabundance of Fire or too little Earth. To determine a person's Elemental state, one can make a list of personality traits. List all the person's positive traits and negative traits and then view each category and its relationship to the Four Elements. If there is an abundance of one correspondence and only a few of another, then one might be looking at an Elemental imbalance. This will provide a fairly accurate assessment of one's Elemental nature.

When working with Elemental natures, it is important to determine which Elements are required to restore a balance. The rule of thumb is Water liberates Earth, Earth gives form to Water, Air gives life to Fire, and Fire gives focus to Air. When too much of one Element is present, it can be released by introducing its complimentary Element. The following is a sample list of positive and negative attributes.

Earth	Air	Fire	Water
+ Strength	+ Creative	+ Energetic	+ Adaptable
+ Endurance	+ Artistic	+ Motivated	+ Changeable
+ Steadfast	+ Intelligent	+ Dynamic	+ Compassionate
- Stubborn	- Flighty	- Combative	- Melancholy
- Lazy	- Distracted	- Destructive	- Pessimistic
- Dominating	- Paranoid	- Violent	- Stagnate

In a magickal context, each of the Elemental energies can be drawn and condensed within the human body for use as a personal power.

Magickal Uses of the Four Elements

There are four basic concepts useful in creating magickal influences related to the Four Elements of Earth, Air, Fire, and Water. Both the astral and physical actions of the Elements should be incorporated into a spell or other work of magick. Fire works through combustion, Water through mixture, Air through evaporation, and Earth through decomposition. These aspects not only empower and transform, but they also connect one's spell to the forces of nature and thus to the connected forces of the supernatural. After spell casting or ritual work, you may have some material left over to dispose (wax, ashes, and so forth), and it is quite effective to use one of the Elemental methods to dispose of them.

If your magick was intended to influence a situation, then the Earth Element is best employed. If it was to accomplish a specific goal, then Fire is a good source of motivation and energy. Romantic works are best connected with the Element of Water. Any matter concerning mental creativity or thoughts in general is best accomplished by employing the Element of Air. It is important to look at all aspects concerning the intended outcome. Break it down into Elemental qualities and employ something symbolic for each related Element. You will generally find that two or more Elements will be required to accomplish your magickal goal. The physical representation of an Element when working a spell is actually a focal point for accessing its astral counterpart.

The following examples will help you understand how to use an object associated with the appropriate element:

Fire: Take a piece of paper or cloth and moisten it with three drops of the universal condenser described in the following section of this chapter. Place this in front of you and concentrate on the desired effect of your magick. Strongly imagine your thoughts pouring into the material, filling it with both your energy and Elemental energy. Imagine your thoughts "writing" your desire across the material. When you sense that your concentration is breaking, the material is fully saturated and you can stop focusing. Now, simply burn the cloth or paper in an open fire. While it is burning, concentrate and visualize the end result of your desire. The fire releases the charge and merges it with the Element. The Element will then carry it into the astral level where it will take root.

Air: Fill a small metal pot about half full with clean water. Add three drops of universal condenser to the water. Put the container over a flame and concentrate upon your desire as you gaze into the water. As the steam rises, visualize what you desire. Once you have the image projected into the steam, your desire is drawn up and carried off. Continue concentrating on the desired outcome until all the water has evaporated.

Water: Fill a container about half full with fresh water. Add three drops of universal condenser and three drops of rubbing alcohol (to connect with vaporous spirits). Now, bestow the water with your concentrated desire, inhale very slowly and deeply, and then exhale out upon the water's surface. Imagine your desire flowing out into the water. When you feel that the water is fully charged, pour it into a stream, river, or any moving body of water.

Earth: You may use either sand or garden soil. Ideally, you want to pick a spot connected to the desired outcome. If the spell is intended for a person, then the soil should be somewhere they will pass by on foot. If the spell is intended for a situation, you may want to sprinkle some of the soil in the setting. You may even consider potting a plant in the charged soil. In this way, you can easily transport it to the target without anyone the wiser. The first step is to add three drops of universal condenser to a pint of mineral water as you concentrate on the desired outcome. Then pour out the mineral water over a selected spot of earth. This will allow the charge to be absorbed directly into the Element of Earth. Place both palms down upon the soil so that the index fingers and thumbs of both hands are touching the wet earth. Picture this as enclosing the area of wet soil between your hands. Conclude by performing the breathing charge as described for the Element of Water.

Elemental Condensers

Condensers are prepared fluids used to carry magickal charges. One way to charge them is by placing your hands together, palms facing down, with the tips of your index fingers and thumbs touching. If done properly, you will form a triangle in the opening between your hands. Inhale deeply, visualizing the Full Moon above your head. Bring the triangle opening in your hands over the condenser liquid and exhale three times through the opening and upon the liquid. As you do this, visualize the light of the Moon pouring down through your head and into your lungs (as you inhale) and then visualize it flowing out with your breath as you exhale.

It is always wise to prepare bottles containing Elemental charges so that you have them when needed. Amber-colored bottles are best because they dilute light entering through the glass. Sunlight will deplete astral charges and your magickal liquids are best kept away from it as much as possible. Other types of colored glass tend to pass on the charge of the color, while amber is neutral and will not contaminate a pure or specific charge.

Once charged, an Elemental condenser can be used to empower a spell or ritual tool. Letters can be anointed with them to convey a specific feel. Statues can also be anointed for ritual work or spell casting. One example would be to take a Faery figurine and anoint it with an Air condenser. The statue can then be used to invoke a Faery spirit or simply to empower a faery magick spell. Ritual tools can be charged with the Element they represent for additional power as well. Traditionally, the pentacle represents Earth, the wand is Air, the athame represents Fire, and the chalice is Water.

Simple Condenser

This condenser can be used to stimulate one's psychic nature and improve clairvoyance. To make this condenser, take two level teaspoons each of chamomile flowers and eyebright and place them in a bowl. Boil two cups of water on an open flame and then add the herbs. Set the mixture aside to cool for fifteen minutes. Then filter the mixture through four layers of clean linen cloth or cheesecloth.

For clairvoyance, soak two cotton balls, close your eyes, and place them upon your eyes for about twenty minutes. To increase psychometric abilities, place a cotton pad on the palms of your hands for the same period of time. A simple condenser can also be drunk as a tea before employing a form of divination such as tarot cards or rune stones.

Universal Condenser

The purpose of this condenser is to accomplish magickal effects upon not only the Material Plane but also the mental and astral levels. Traditionally, this compound is used to create artificial Elementals (serving spirits), to empower magick mirrors and to animate paintings for use as portals or in meditation. This method uses the Lunar Mansion charge in which the liquid is charged over a period of twenty-eight days, beginning with the Moon in Aries. Check a good astrological calendar for this timing.

Take equal parts of the following ingredients:

- Angelica (Spirit)
- Tobacco (Earth)
- Mint (Air)
- Cinnamon (Fire)
- Watermelon (Water)

Add this mixture to a half quart of boiling water and boil for twenty minutes. Strain the water through cheesecloth. Pour the filtered water into a bowl and let cool. Next, pour about two ounces of a Frangelico Liquore into the bowl.

Then, secure a piece of silver jewelry from a chain and heat it in an open flame until it is very hot. Next, dip the jewelry into the bowl. If you made the jewelry hot enough, you should hear it hiss as it enters the liquid. Remove the silver piece and add three drops of your own blood to the mixture. Finally, pour this into amber-colored bottles for later use. Add water for a fifty-fifty mixture and cap the bottles. Place the bottle out at night beneath the Full Moon for added charging. This can and should be performed each Full Moon. The condensers are used in future chapters.

Earth Condenser

Chop up a small piece of parsley. Crush a pinch of caraway seed and add it to the parsley. Slice up three petals from a carnation flower and mix all together. Then heat up two ounces of olive oil and pour the mixture into it. Let simmer for twenty minutes. Strain the oil through a layer of cheese-cloth and pour the filtered oil into a bottle. Add three drops of tincture of benzoin compound to keep the oil from spoiling. This tincture is available at most pharmacies. Label the prepared oil and charge it with the Element.

Air Condenser

Crush three juniper berries and three hazel nuts. Slice up three rose petals and three leaves from a cherry tree. You can substitute with the stems from a cherry if you cannot obtain the leaves. Prepare the oil as prescribed for the Earth condenser. Pour the oil into a bottle, label it, and perform the Elemental charge.

Fire Condenser

Chop up a very small amount (equal parts) of garlic and onion. Crush a pinch of mustard seeds and add this with a pinch of pepper to the garlic and onion. Add to prepared oil as described, bottle, and charge the oil.

Water Condenser

Crush a small slice of a turnip and a sugar beet. Add three sliced peony blossoms along with three cherry tree leaves (or cherry stems). Add to prepared oil as described, bottle, and charge it.

After spell casting or ritual magick, you will have some material left over such as wax or ashes which you will need to dispose in the proper manner. Each remnant will have an Elemental correspondence with which you can associate it. Simply use one of the Elemental methods to complete the magickal process. The Earth Element will govern works associated with people and situations. Fire governs goal-reaching and works of motivation, passion, or destruction. The Water Element governs romantic and emotional works. Air governs matters concerning mental creativity and thought processes in general.

The Four Directional Quarters

Many cultures have regarded the compass points of North, East, South, and West as sacred directions. In the magickal and ritual arts, the four directions are also considered portals or gateways between the Spirit Realm and the world of the living.

Ritual circles in which practitioners gather are designed with a marker at each directional quarter. The most common marker is a candle. In many systems of ritual and magick, a tower is envisioned at each quarter and is known as a Watchtower. Some systems assign Elemental lords or kings to each tower. Other systems view the Watchers as stellar beings, elementals, or even as angels.

The basic view is that the portals are connected to the Elemental Plane of Forces. These doorways or gates open "between the worlds;" that is to say, between the declared boundary of the marked ritual circle and the "other side" of reality. Many traditions envision guardians at each of these interfacing points at the four quarters within a ritual circle. This concept appears in the illustrations below.

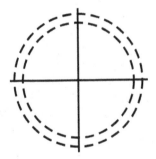

The inner corridor appears when the circle is created by the Elemental Forces. When properly evoked, the Elemental Forces flow to and from the circle, which is depicted in the illustration by the tips of the Elemental cross penetrating the edge of the marked circle. The outer circle is the membrane between us and the Elemental Plane.

The Elemental Forces become contained within the cast circle and are available to the ritualist in this setting. In other words, the Elements are at hand. In effect, the ritualist becomes the Fifth Element that governs the creative Elements. Through this, the ritualist can create a "mini-universe" of her or his own—a microcosm.

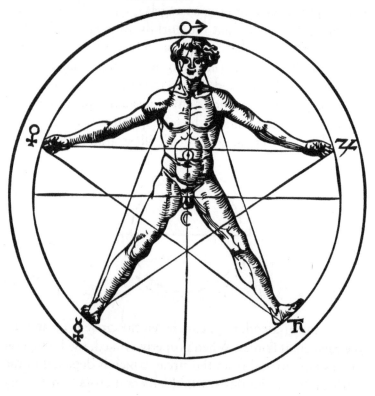

The ritual or magickal circle is, in true regard, the Universe of the ritualist. It is here that magickal energy is gathered and formed into something cohesive, which can receive a special desire or intention. Once the "thought" is passed into an energy-form, it can be directed into the Elemental Plane. This in turn will move the energy into the Astral Realm, and there all thoughts and desires can become manifest by passing back into the Material Realm. This is covered in detail in Chapter Six.

Each of the four quarters is assigned a nature of metaphysical correspondence. The North is often thought of as the place of power. The keyword for North is manifestation. It is a stabilizing, fortifying, and enduring emanation of force. To open the portal to the North is to be washed in that energy.

The East is considered the place of conveyance. The keyword for the East is transmission. It is a cerebral, etheric, spiritual, and communicating force. To open the portal to the East is to bring yourself into this emanation.

The South is envisioned as the place of change. Its keyword is transformation. It is activating, enlivening, and altering. To open the portal to the South is to join in the shift from material to non-material.

The West is thought of as the place of flow. The keyword for the West is movement. It is carrying, coursing, and running. To open the portal to the West is to enter the stream or current itself.

Chapter One Test

1. What is the name of the ancient Greek credited with creating a cohesive teaching of the Four Elements?

2. What is the Fifth Element?

3. What is the dominant force of Earth?

4. What is the dominant force of Air?

5. What is the dominant force of Fire?

6. What is the dominant force of Water?

7. In the context of this lesson, what does the pentagram represent?

8. What is the magickal nature of Earth?

9. What is the magickal nature of Air?

10. What is the magickal nature of Fire?

11. What is the magickal nature of Water?

12. What is another title for the Elemental Plane?

13. What is the tonal sound associated with the following Elements:

    - Earth:
    - Air:
    - Fire:
    - Water:

14. What beings are associated with each of the Four Elements?

    - Earth:
    - Air:
    - Fire:
    - Water:

Chapter II

Using the Pentacle

In the magickal arts, we find the altar tool known as the pentacle. It represents the Material Realm as well as the Element of Earth, or more precisely, the Elemental Force of Earth. Traditionally, the pentacle is made of clay, stone, or metal. These materials come directly from the earth, which links the tool to the Elemental Nature.

The origins of the pentacle may lie in the use of gourds, which in turn were displaced by wooden platters or flat rocks. For example, in the ancient Cult of Mithras, a platter was used as one of four ritual tools. The others were a cup, wand, and a metal blade. A scourge and a "sun whip" were also used in the Cult, and collectively these tools resemble those appearing centuries later in Gardnerian-inspired Witchcraft.

The pentacle, in its connection to the Element of Earth, is primarily used for the purpose of manifestation. In connection to this theme, the tool is also used to declare the magickal or ritual work at hand. For example, once a ritual circle has been cast, the pentacle can be carried around its perimeter while declaring the circle as a barrier, container, and protective boundary.

The pentacle can also serve to open and close gateways or portals at the four directional quarters of the circle: North, East, South, and West. In this usage, the pentacle is held in the hands as pictured below and is pivoted like a door. Moving and swinging the pentacle away from you is an opening gesture and moving it back towards you is the gesture of closing. Focus on the sensation of a physical door opening or closing.

As an altar tool, the pentacle is often marked with the magickal and sacred symbols of the group (or solitary practitioner). This serves to connect the material with the non-material realms (the Physical Realm and the Metaphysical Realm). This embraces the concept of "as above, so below" in the respect that the symbols unite what they represent in terms of earthly adherence. In other words, the symbols represent the spiritual markers of the group or individual and reflect them into the ritual setting and mindset of the practitioners. One example is the pentacle that is often ascribed to Gardnerian Witchcraft.

In this example, the center star represents the Four Elements under the influence of the Fifth Element known as Spirit or Aether. This speaks to the power of manifestation in accord with personal will or desire. It signifies the pentacle as a tool whereby form is given and maintained. Above the star, from left to right, are the symbols of the degrees of initiation. These are the levels of attainment in understanding the ritual and magickal arts. Near the lower tips of the star appear the symbol of the divine masculine (left) and the divine feminine (right). These unite the symbolism of the pentacle with the concept of fertility, which in turn allows for manifestation. Beneath the star appears the symbol of the kiss and the scourge, which denote passion and endurance. These are signs of devotion and dedication as well as catalysts to altered states of consciousness.

From a spiritual perspective, the pentacle is symbolic of the shield carried by the spiritual warrior. In this context, it is sometimes called the "Shield of Valor." The idea here is that personal ethics and self-knowledge provides the strength of character necessary to persevere on one's path. Nothing can undo or take away a steadfast position that is built upon a strong and true foundation. In this sense, the pentacle symbolizes the practitioner as an unconquerable guardian against all that is unbalanced, untruthful, and deconstructive.

Charging the Pentacle

There are several ways to use the pentacle in magick and ritual. Naturally, you will need to obtain or make one. It is most effective to use one made from clay or metal. However, a wooden pentacle can also be effective since it aligns with the Element of Earth, which is tied to the Greenwood Realm of Nature. Avoid synthetic materials.

Ideally, your pentacle should be no larger than a standard dinner plate and no smaller than a saucer (such as used to serve a cup of coffee or tea). The pentacle needs to have a pentagram marked upon it. As previously mentioned, this connection to the Four Elements, coupled with its role as an Elemental tool, grants the pentacle its power from the Material Plane. In other words, it serves you in manifesting your intentions.

Once you have your physical pentacle, take it outdoors at noon. Cover it with a layer of soil (potting soil is fine). Around the pentacle, mark a triangle using either pebbles or lines of soil (enclosing the pentacle in the center of the triangle). Next, place the palms of both hands over the pentacle and say these words:

> *"I declare this pentacle to be a tool through which the forces of Elemental Earth can be attracted, drawn, focused, and wielded."*

Next, form the Triangle of Manifestation by joining both hands together as pictured below. Place this over the buried pentacle so that you see the center of the area through the opening between the hands.

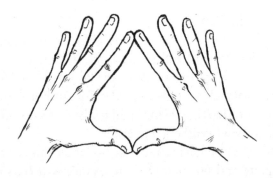

Focus your attention on the Element of Earth. Sense your body becoming solid and firm like a boulder. Breath in deeply three times and sense this feeling become stronger each time. Now it is time to pass this vibration into the pentacle beneath the soil. To do this, you will give a tonal, which is the sound of the alphabet letter "A." Direct the sound of your voice through the Triangle and into the pentacle. Begin by first saying the following words and then passing the tonal as described:

"By the tonal of Earth, I pass into this
pentacle the quality of Earth, and I establish
the principle of like attracts like. Thereby I create
this Elemental pentacle of Earth."

Now, sound the letter a, stretching it out in your exhaled breath in this manner:

"Aaaaaaaaa."

Lastly, trace the entire star on the pentacle from its upper tip and back again, saying these words of empowerment:

"Strict charge and watch I give, that in the
presence of this pentacle, nothing evil, negative,
or imbalanced may approach or enter in."

Using the Pentacle

In this section, we will look at several ways to use the pentacle in ritual and magick. To begin, let us consider its use in casting a circle. Prior to setting your circle, carry the pentacle around the perimeter (beginning at the North). As you move around the circle, hold the pentacle out in front of you with both hands. Face the star symbol away from you and towards the outside of the circle. Say these words as you pass around inside the circle (one full and complete round):

> *"Behold the pentacle, wielder of Elemental*
> *Earth. What is cast this day is bound this day,*
> *as above so below."*

(This announces that the circle is to be set in accord with the Force of Earth and will hold the properties of protection and containment.)

Once completed, set the pentacle of the altar. After you have finished casting your circle per your method, you can use the pentacle to open (and later close) portals to the four directions. This is accomplished by going to each quarter, beginning with the East, and holding the pentacle outward to the rim of the circle. Think of this posture as though you are holding the hatch to a round window on a ship. The hatch swings out to open the view and inward to close it. Use the pentacle in that manner. Be sure always to close any and all portals that you open.

When using the pentacle as a hatchway, you can say words to this effect:

> *"By the power of the pentacle, I open this portal*
> *between the worlds and connect the world of*
> *mortal kind with that of the Otherworld."*

To close the portal, say:

> *"By the power of the pentacle, I close this portal*
> *between the worlds and disconnect the world of*
> *mortal kind from that of the Otherworld."*

The pentacle can be used as a focal point that bring about manifestation on the Physical Plane. It is like a magickal platter. To use it in this way, place an object that you wish to empower or enchant. The pentacle represents manifestation and is like a homing device for Elemental Earth. One example is the charging of a ring for some magickal purpose such as protection.

Place the ring on the center of the pentacle. Speak these words of enchantment as you trace the entire five-pointed star on the pentacle from the upper tip downward to the right and follow the lines back again to the upper tip of the star:

> *"I evoke the essence of Divine Spirit and invoke its protective nature into this ring."*

Then trace the entire star from its Earth position up to the tip and around the entire pentagram back to the Earth position, saying:

> *"I evoke the essence of Earth, and I invoke its fortifying nature into this ring."*

One last example of using the pentacle is to bind something or someone from abusive or mean-spirited action. To do this, take something that links to the person, such as a photo, clip of hair, item of clothing, jewelry, etc. This will be placed beneath the pentacle for one full cycle of the Moon (beginning as the Moon wanes from Full).

Begin by placing the pentacle on your altar to the left side and the object off to the right. Trace the star from the Earth position and back again, saying:

> *"I evoke the power of Earth to bind, to enclose,*
> *to cease activity."*

Next, pick up the pentacle and hold it over the personal item, and say:

> *"I direct the power of Earth to bind you,*
> *enclose you away from [name the person or*
> *situation], and stop your actions."*

Then slowly lower the pentacle down on to the item. Do this with focused intent, and deliberate intention. Use words to this effect:

> *"The weight of Earth overpowers you,*
> *holds you still, ceases your ill intentions, and*
> *stops your harmful actions. You are held bound*
> *from harming others. Be still, be silent."*

Leave the pentacle in place until the Full Moon and then remove the object beneath it. You may need to repeat this if problems persist.

The Elemental Star

As should be apparent from this and the previous chapter, the pentacle is the center of operation within the ritual or magickal circle. Through the use of the pentacle, you can interface with any of the Elements, draw and direct them, and use them to create magickal energy to manifest your desires or intentions.

By using the Elemental points of the star (as pictured in this lesson), you can evoke or invoke the forces of Earth, Air, Fire, and Water. This is done by holding up the pentacle in one hand at the corresponding quarter position in the circle: North (Earth), East (Air), South (Fire), and West (Water). Then use the other hand to trace the star in accord with the assigned Elemental Force of each quarter. In other words, begin tracing from the tip of the star that marks the appropriate Elemental nature.

To enhance this, you can first trace the star in its elemental pattern and then swing the pentacle to the open position. Remember to close after the ritual or magickal work. Also, bear in mind that any evoked or invoked Element must be released and banished so that it does not linger and create an imbalance on the Material Realm.

Use the Elemental chart that follows for the traditional methods of calling and releasing these Forces.

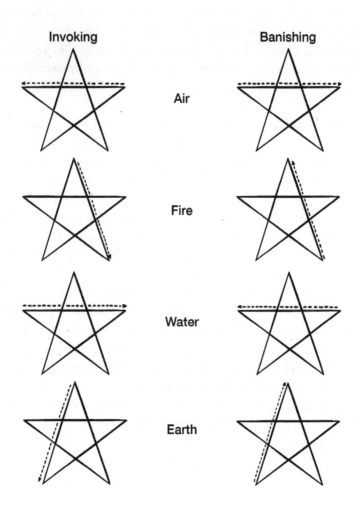

Invoking   Banishing

Air

Fire

Water

Earth

Chapter Two Test

1. What materials are pentacles made of traditionally?

2. What is one use of the pentacle at a ritual quarter?

3. What is the purpose of marking additional symbols besides the five-pointed star on the pentacle?

4. Which device of the Spiritual Warrior is represented by the pentacle?

5. What does the five-pointed star on the pentacle represent?

6. What is the Tonal Sound for each of the Four Elements?

- Earth:
- Air:
- Fire:
- Water:

7. How does the pentacle draw or attract the Element of Earth?

8. Why can the pentacle be considered the Center of Operation within a ritual or magickal circle?

9. What is intended by carrying the pentacle around the area where the ritual or magickal circle is to be set?

10. What does the "Elemental Star" on the pentacle symbolize in addition to reflecting the Four Elements?

Chapter Three

Using the Wand

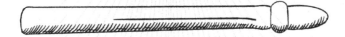

The wand is among the most ancient tools used by ritualists and magicians of the past. It has a rich history that will be explored in this chapter. Ancient classical writings depict Witches such as *Medea* using a wand for magickal purposes. Over the centuries, the wand is depicted in relationship to the wizard and sorceress as well. Among the earliest references, wands were commonly made from beech tree.

There is an archaic spiritual tradition associated with trees, and, by extension, with wands. It is connected to the sacred groves venerated by our ancestors. Tree worship was common in antiquity. Each grove contained a sacred tree central to the cult. Its branches held special meaning as is evidenced by ancient tales of the sacred bough. One example is the *Silver Bough* of northern European lore, which is connected to the Faery Realm. Another example is the *Golden Bough* of southern European lore, which is associated with the Underworld. In this lore, the essential item required to successfully complete a quest is provided through magickal means linked to a tree.

To carry a sacred bough was to wield the power of the force, entity, or deity within it. Therefore, it was considered essential to establish a personal rapport. In associated lore, the priestess or priest trained in service to the spirit of the sacred tree. The years spent in this way came to represent the measurement of their devotion, service, alignment, and rapport. Once a period of time was served, the priestess or priest was allowed to take a branch from the tree. This branch became the staff, a sign of mastery and devotion.

The branch reflected the skill of the priestess or priest. It was cut to match the individuals height, plus the length from the inside of the elbow to the tip of the middle finger. The former symbolized the experience of the priestess or priest, while the latter represented the service of the priestess or priest to their Community. In this way, the wand is the bridge to and from the Divine through the conduit of those in service.

According to old lore, when the One God came to displace the Many, the Old Ways went into hiding. Over time, the staff diminished into the wand, still retaining its symbolic connection to a sacred grove and to its Divine Nature. This is one of the reasons why the wand is traditionally made of wood, for this roots it in its lineage. In contemporary wands, some practitioners choose to make them of metal, stone, or other substances.

The Elemental Nature

In some systems, the wand is assigned to the Element of Fire and, in others, it is associated with air. The assignment of Fire may be rooted in the ancestral knowledge of using friction on wood to ignite a fire. The old lore held that fire was inside wood and could be evoked from it. Later in time, a glass lens was used to coax out the fire. This was one method of passing the Divine Flame of a grove from one site to another. To accomplish this, bundles of branches were carried off to another area. These branches served not only to pass on the original sacred fire from the sacred tree, but also provided the first supply of torches for the new grove.

Now let us look at the alternative Elemental alignment. The assignment of Air with the wand is rooted in the nature of the branch, which swayed in the breeze. The branch was also the resting place of birds (creatures of the air) and a site for building their nests. In the mystical sense, the wand is coaxed to "remember" its movement in the wind and thus become animated by air.

In some systems, the wand is connected to the mental will of an individual and, in others, it is the intuition. The wand is directional in its concept and connected to Elemental Forces that evoke and invoke. This theme relates to the principle of the mind's ability to visualize thoughts that can become forms. This is reflected in the imagery of the Magician card in the tarot.

The Magician in tarot is connected to Mercury, the planet and the Greek god Hermes. The wand of Hermes is the Caduceus, the rod with two entwined serpents. Hermes was, among other things, the messenger of the gods bearing his "wand of miracles." As such, he was the transmitter and channel, which is still reflected in the Elemental Nature of the wand.

In ritual, an altar is the focal point of the circle, which is the microcosm of the Universe, the Magician's world within the greater world. Here, the Magician calls up the Four Elements and creates a sphere containing forces drawn to or raised within it. It is part Elemental Force and part material resonance. It is literally between the Worlds.

In the tarot imagery, the Magician raises his wand upward

THE MAGICIAN.

to the heights with one hand and directs his intention downward to the depths with the other. Upon the altar is the staff (along with other tools of the Art). Here, the Magician stands as the Sacred Tree bearing the branch that is his measure.

Ritual and Magickal Uses of the Wand

The wand has a variety of uses in ritual and magick. It can be used to cast a circle with, control open portal activity, direct energy that is drawn or raised, and pass blessings to a setting, person, or group of individuals. In this light, it is also used to bless ritual cakes and wine on the altar. All of this is connected to the link between the divine and the wand, and its nature to be a bridge or conduit.

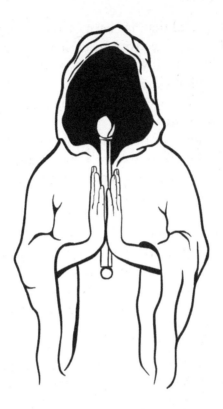

In a ritual circle, the wand can be used to announce the beginning or end of a rite. This is done by simply knocking on the surface of the altar with the end of the wand. Traditionally, three such knocks are sounded. The same technique can be used to declare that a ritual or magickal circle has been properly cast. In essence, the wand represents the authority of the Divine.

As a tool of authority, the wand can be raised upward or outward to command. It can also be carried around a ritual or magickal that has been cast to enforce the nature of the circle as a protective barrier. In its magickal aspect, a wand held horizontally blocks or signals a stop, while one held upright allows entry or passage. This makes the wand effective in front of open portals or gateways left temporarily open into the ritual circle.

Another aspect of the wand is its connection with the theme of fertility. If we picture a mortar and pestle set, we can liken it to a wand and chalice. In a ritual and magickal sense, the wand is a phallus and the chalice is a womb. Inserting the wand into the chalice is an act of procreation, a ritual or magickal act designed to impregnate and bring forth offspring. The offspring, in this case, is the end result of a spell or the manifested intention of a ritual.

For the blessing of ritual cakes and wine, the wand is used to trace a symbol over the sacred meal. This symbol can be unique to the practitioner (with symbolic significance) or can be something general like a crescent for lunar blessings and a circle for solar. The presence and manipulation of the wand awakens the spiritual essence of the wine as the blood of the divine feminine, and the cake as the flesh of the divine masculine. In some systems, this is reversed.

Symbolism of the Wand

Various symbols can be placed along the sides of the wand. Ideally, these should include symbols of deities and spirits that the practitioner works with in ritual and magick. Other symbols can include Elemental connections.

With the wand held in hand, the symbols become affirmations and alignments flowing through the consciousness of the wielder. Symbols are a form of language for entities on the other side. They not only convey intention and the source of power, they also become energetic thought-forms. In other words, they have impact through the power they represent, and thereby a reaction to them is made manifest.

The symbols for the wand can be painted, carved, drawn, or even burned on with a wood-burning tool. While placing each symbol on the wand, focus your mind on its meaning. Once in place, trace your finger over the symbol and verbally declare what it represents.

Elemental Charging of the Wand

In this section, you will find two methods of charging the wand. One method aligns the tool to the Element of Air and the other connects it with the Element of Fire. Simply choose which Element you feel is most connected to the wand and then use the corresponding Elemental charge.

To Charge by Air

Light a blue candle and some incense with a flowery scent. Pass the wand through the flame three times, each time saying these words:

"Through the transformational force of Fire, I change this tool from a mere physical item into a magickal implement."

Now, stand with your wand in your left hand. Stretch both arms up so that your body forms the letter "Y" (feet together and arms extended). Imagine you are a tree and then gently move your arms like branches swaying in the wind. Try and connect with this feeling of moving air that causes your motion. This will establish a connection between you, the wand, and the Element of Air.

The next step is to pass the Element of Air into the wand. While holding the wand in your left hand, use the index finger of your right hand over the wand to trace the five-pointed star in the direction pictured below, moving from the starting point and back again. In other words, trace the entire figure above the wand, passing the force of Air into it.

Do this three times. To enhance this technique, blow your breath across the wand each time prior to tracing the pentagram over it.

Next, pass the wand through the incense smoke, saying:

"Be you the summoner,
the stirrer of mystical Air."

Finally, wrap the wand in a cloth and suspend it with a cord tied to a tree branch. Do this preferably on the night of a Full Moon. If circumstances prevent you from using a tree, then suspend the wand in your home somewhere (a temporary hook in the ceiling or door frame will serve nicely). Leave the wand suspended for the night. It is then ready to use.

To Charge by Fire
Light a red-colored candle and some spicy incense such as cinnamon. Pass the wand through the candle flame three times, saying:

"Through the transformational force of Fire, I
change this tool from a mere physical item into a
magickal implement."

The next step is to pass the Element of Fire into the wand. While holding the wand in your left hand, use the index finger of your right hand over the wand to trace the five-pointed star in the direction pictured below, moving from the starting point and back again. In other words, trace the entire figure above the wand, passing the force of fire into it.

Next, hold the tip of the wand in front of your eyes so that it blocks out the flame and you see the glow behind it from the candle. Slowly lower the wand so that the flame appears to sit upon the tip of the wand. You can experiment with closing one eye to achieve this effect.

Imagine the wand as a magickal torch that can bear a flame or take one back into it. Move the wand up and down slowly so you see the flame appear and disappear. Once you can do this smoothly, repeat the process three times, saying these words:

> *"Wand, you bearer of the Mystic Flame, bring forth its force and draw it in again."*

The wand is now ready to use. In the meantime, wrap it in a red cloth or tie a red ribbon around it.

Portals and the Wand

In a previous chapter, we looked at the pentacle as a type of hatch or door for each of the portals: North, East, South, and West. The wand can be used in conjunction with the pentacle or used alone for the purpose of controlling what passes or approaches the portals of a ritual or magickal circle.

Whenever a portal into another realm is opened, it becomes a two-way channel. It is for this reason the wand is used to direct and control all activity. The tip of the wand is the directional operative, and the shaft is the key that locks or unlocks. As mentioned earlier, when the wand is held vertical, it allows passage. When it is held out horizontally, it blocks passage or stops activity. Try rotating the wand in your hand, upright and then sideways, to become comfortable with the ritual gesture. It is helpful to imagine the wand as a key, locking and unlocking.

In terms of directing with the wand, it is much like a flashlight in the dark to scan an area. The difference is that the wand directs instead of reveals. So, switch to this idea when using the wand and you can get a feel for its directional use. In this way, the wand is ideal for evoking, invoking, and banishing.

In the chapter on rituals, you will find various techniques for using the wand along with the "calls" to the Quarter Portals.

Chapter Three Test

1. What is one of the earliest trees from which wands were made?

2. Why were trees worshipped in ancient times?

3. What was the significance of carrying a staff from the Sacred Grove in ancient tradition?

4. What does the body measure from the inside of the elbow to the tip of the index represent in the wand's length?

5. Why is the wand associated with Elemental Air?

6. Why is the wand associated with Elemental Fire?

7. How is the wand held to open and to close portals?

8. What does the wand represent when placed within a chalice?

9. How is the wand used to announce the beginning or ending of something in a ritual setting?

10. What is the key idea behind the wand in magickal use?

Chapter Four

Using the athame

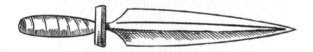

The use of a knife in ritual and magick is a very ancient practice. It is mentioned in pre-Christian literature and in books on magick and ritual over the centuries. In European occult traditions, the blade is double-edged, symbolizing that it operates within both material reality and non-material reality. It is perhaps the most formidable tools at the practitioner's command.

The traditional athame has a black handle, which represents the procreative state of existence from which all things issue forth. It is black because black is the presence of all colors combined. This symbolizes the ability to open any single aspect of blackness. Black is also the color of the night, and in this way, the athame is connected to spirits of the night. Among the four ritual tools, the athame is the most "forceful" or "commanding" in nature and is used when this energy is needed in ritual or magick.

Similarly to the wand, some systems assign the athame to Air and others to Fire. As a tool of Fire, the athame is aligned to transformation, and as a tool of Air, it is connected to the personal will and the mind. In the case of the latter, the athame is the "sword of discernment" and serves to cut away illusion. The athame has power as a blade in material reality and non-material reality. Its mystical presence is just as powerful as its physical one.

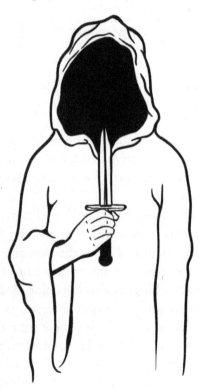

On the Material Plane, the athame is never used for physical carving, cutting, or mundane acts. In its place, the boline knife is used. Traditionally, this knife has a white handle. It is also the traditional blade used for harvesting herbs.

Basic Charging of the Athame

In some Western occult traditions, charging an athame requires the use of fire and a lodestone (a natural magnet). To begin, place a bowl of water and a lighted candle on your work area. Next, heat the metal blade with the candle flame for a couple of minutes (focus on the tip). When the blade is very hot, say:

"Blade of steel, I conjure thee!"

Then hold the blade over the water, and right before you plunge it into the water, say

"Banish all things as named by me!"

When the blade meets the water, you should hear a sizzling sound.

The next step is to magnetize the athame. Begin by drying off the blade with a cloth. Then, hold the handle in one hand and the magnet in the other. Stroke the magnet in one direction (not back and forth) from the tip of the blade down to the handle. You will need to do this at least thirty times. As you stroke the blade, repeat these words:

> *"Blade of steel I conjure thee,*
> *attract all things as name by me."*

When finished, wrap the athame in a cloth and leave it overnight.

Elemental Charging of Athame

In this section, you will find two methods of charging the athame. One method aligns the tool to the Element of Air and the other connects it with the Element of Fire. Simply choose which Element you feel most connects to the athame and then use the corresponding Elemental charge.

To Charge by Air

Light a blue candle and some incense with a flowery scent. Pass the athame through the flame three times, each time saying these words:

> *"Through the transformational force of Fire, I change this tool from a mere physical item into a magickal implement."*

Now, stand with your athame in your left hand and stretch both arms outward so your body forms a cross (feet together and arms extended). Imagine standing on the edge of a cliff and sense the feeling of a breeze blowing past you. Try and feel the moving air brushing over you. This will establish a connection between you, the athame, and the Element of Air.

Now, point your athame into the imagined breeze. Blow your breath over the athame, from handle to tip. Do this three times. Then, quickly and firmly swing the blade back and forth. Try to create the sound of the blade whipping through the air.

The next step is to pass the Element of Air into the athame. While holding the athame in your left hand, use the index finger of your right hand over the blade to trace the five-pointed star in the direction pictured below, moving from the starting point and back again. In other words, trace the entire star-figure above the athame, passing the force of Air into it.

Do this three times. To enhance this technique, blow your breath across the blade each time prior to tracing the pentagram over it.

Next, pass the athame through the incense smoke, saying:

"Be you the summoner, the stirrer
of mystical Air."

Once this is completed, wrap it in a cloth and suspend it with a cord tied to a tree branch. Do this preferably on the night of a Full Moon. If circumstances prevent you from using a tree, then suspend the athame in your home some-where (a temporary hook in the ceiling or door frame will serve nicely). Leave the athame suspended for the night. It is then ready to use.

To Charge by Fire

Light a red-colored candle and some spicy incense such as cinnamon. Pass the athame through the candle flame three times, saying:

> *"Through the transformational force of Fire, I change this tool from a mere physical item into a magickal implement."*

The next step is to pass the Element of Fire into the athame. While holding it in your left hand, use the index finger of your right hand over the athame to trace the five-pointed star in the direction pictured below, moving from the starting point and back again. In other words, trace the entire star-figure above the athame, passing the force of Fire into it.

Next, hold the tip of the athame in front of your eyes so that it blocks out the flame and you see the glow behind it from the candle. Slowly lower the athame so that the flame appears to sit upon the tip of the athame. You can experiment with closing one eye to achieve this effect.

Imagine the athame to be a magickal torch that can bear a flame or take one back into it. Move the blade up and down slowly so you see the flame appear and disappear. Once you can do this smoothly, repeat the process three times, saying these words:

> *"Athame, you bearer of the Mystic Flame, bring forth its force and draw it in again."*

Finish the charge by standing with arms down at each side, the athame in the right hand. In your mind, picture flames shooting up from a bonfire. Sense yourself as fire and then quickly thrust both arms upward as though they are jetting flames (be careful with the blade). Repeat this three times.

The athame is now ready to use. In the meantime, wrap it in a red cloth or tie a red ribbon around it.

Using the Athame

In ritual, the primary use of the athame is to cast a circle. As a tool of Fire, it transforms the mundane into the magickal. As a tool of Air, it focuses the will of the practitioner to manifest a demarcation. In this usage, the athame is pointed downward as the practitioner walks around the edge of the circle area. In effect, the athame is tracing an energy line to mark the perimeter of the circle. Once a circle is established, the athame can be used to "cut" an opening in its perimeter, which allows a practitioner to enter and exit while keeping the force field in place. The perimeter field will seal itself once the athame is removed from the edge of the circle.

The athame is also used to direct energy into objects and settings within a ritual (a task shared by the wand as well). Spirits are responsive to the presence and the physical manipulation of the athame. This is because the athame represents not only the Elemental Force wielded by the practitioner, but also because of its connection to the personal will of the individual.

In some traditions, the athame represents the divine masculine force and is used along with the chalice, which symbolizes the divine feminine. One example is the Wiccan ceremony known as the Great Rite. In Pagan tradition, the athame can also represent the Horned God. In ritual and magick, the athame is regarded as the phallus and the chalice as the womb. During the ritual, the athame is lowered into the chalice in an act that is meant to mimic sexual union. In some magickal traditions, the wand is used in place of the athame.

The athame in modern times is used to evoke the Elements at each quarter of the ritual circle. This is performed by the practitioner standing at each quarter (East, South, West, and North) and tracing the ascribed invoking pentagram in the air. This is done in a continuous sweeping motion. Upon completion of the ritual, this action is repeated using the banishing gestures. (See Page 46.)

Portal Protection

Any doorway, portal, or access point can be blocked using a magickal charge from the athame. This is accomplished by tracing the five-pointed star and then enclosing it in a triple circle. In this usage, the pentagram is not an Elemental one, so don't equate it. Instead, tap into the symbolic representation of the pentagram symbolizing Spirit over the Four Elements of Creation. In this sense, Spirit is an irresistible force or power. Once displayed, that is the principle in motion.

To begin, point the athame at the opening you wish to block or protect. Using the illustration below, you will trace a five-pointed star in the air with a continuous sweeping motion until you return the starting position. As you do this, say these words:

> *"Strict charge and watch I give, that to this place, nothing evil, disharmonious, negative, harmful, or imbalanced may approach nor enter in."*

Upon returning to the top tip of the star, trace three clockwise circles to enclose the star. Then, point your athame directly center in the star and say:

> *"By the power of Spirit over the Four Elements, and in the Light of Divine Emanation, be it so!"*

When you desire to remove or deactivate this force, simply trace the star in the opposite direction and say:

> *"By the power of Spirit over the Four Elements,*
> *I dissolve the forces gathered here, and I withdraw*
> *the Light of Divine Emanation, be it so!"*

Complete by tracing three circles counterclockwise in the air and then slash the air as though cutting something away in front of you.

This entire technique can also be used to charge a ring, bracelet, or necklace with protection.

Chapter Four Test

1. What does the double-edged blade of the athame symbolize?

2. What does the black handle on the athame symbolize?

3. What nature does the Element of Air bring to the athame?

4. What nature does the Element of Fire bring to the athame?

5. What is the athame never used for?

6. What does the use of a lodestone pass to the athame?

7. How is the athame used in the presence of a doorway or portal?

8. How is the athame used in order for the ritual circle to be open or closed?

Chapter Five

Using the Chalice

The tool known as the chalice represents the Element of Water. Its history as a ritual tool goes back to its origins as a shell, gourd, or even a carved wooden bowl. In the beginning, it was likely used more as a simple vessel, but later in time, it took on mystical connections. However, the foundational associations from early periods shaped the chalice as a sacred altar tool. Before looking at the chalice as a ritual object, it will be helpful to reveal its deep spiritual, mystical, and magickal connections. These can be found in the myths and legends of the pre-Christian European people.

The water collected from sacred and magickal sites has been regarded as having special qualities and virtues. The vessel used to transport and contain it is likewise given power through contact with the water. All this shares a relationship with the mythos of the Holy Grail, which, before its arrogation by Christianity, some believe was part of the Goddess Cult of Old Europe.

The oldest vessels constructed by humans and associated with a goddess are the basket and the cauldron. In their design, we find symbols along with myths and legends representing them as cult objects. In the case of the chalice, we find the connection back to the cauldron, which itself shares a sacred mythos (as does the cup in the Grail stories).

The cauldron symbolizes the womb of the Goddess, the vessel of generation and regeneration. It is the life-giver and the receiver of life returned to its origin. The cauldron appears in many tales. In myth and legend, it brews potions, aids in spell casting, produces abundance or decline, and is a holy vessel for offerings to the powers of the night and to the Great Goddess. Its main attribute is that of transformation, either spiritually or physically. As a symbol of the Goddess, it bestows wisdom, knowledge, and inspiration.

One example is found in the tale of the Cauldron of Cerridwen.

The basic story recounts how Cerridwen prepared a brew in her cauldron designed to enlighten her son. The potion had to brew for a year and a day. The story goes that the brew is accidentally tasted by a character called Gwion for whom it was not intended. This angers the Goddess, and she pursues the offender in a lengthy chase. Both Cerridwen and Gwion transform into a series of various animals during the chase. In legend, the Cauldron of Cerridwen was warmed by the breath of nine maidens and produced an elixir that conferred inspiration. This seems to reflect the earlier Greek influence of the Nine Muses who gave inspiration to humans. Noteworthily, in line twenty-seven of the Taliesin riddle (from the Celtic work *The Tale of Taliesin*), we find the words: *"I have obtained the muse from the Cauldron of Cerridwen."* The Muses freed mortals from the drudgery of physical reality and provided access to Eternal Truths.

In the Celtic legends, Cerridwen's cauldron is depicted with a ring of pearls around its rim. It was located in the realm of Annwn (the Underworld) and, according to Taliesin's poem *The Spoils of Annwn*, the fire beneath it was kindled by the breath of nine maidens, from which oracles emerged. This is similar to the Greek Muses, who were connected to the Oracle at Delphi. What is of interest to us here is the association of the cauldron to the Underworld. To understand this connection, we must now look at the Grail Mysteries.

In Taliesin's poem *The Spoils of Annwn,* we encounter a group of adventurers who descend into Annwn to recover the missing cauldron. They locate it in Caer Sidi or Caer Pedryan, the legendary four cornered castle. This is sometimes also known as Castle Spiral. In symbolism, the spiral was, among other things, a tomb symbol representing death and renewal. It is here in the center of the spiral, itself within the center of the castle, that the adventurers find the Cauldron of Cerridwen.

The tale represents many mystery teachings. One aspect concerns itself with the lunar mysteries. Here, the missing cauldron of Cerridwen represents the waning of the Moon and its disappearance for three days (prior to the return of the crescent in the night sky). To the ancients, this was a time of dread for the Moon was gone. It had to be retrieved from the Underworld into which the Moon seemingly descended each night. The quest to retrieve the cauldron of Cerridwen is a quest to retrieve the light of the Moon. The cauldron is the source of that light and belongs to the Goddess. All of this can be extended to the chalice.

Examining the Chalice

As previously noted, the chalice is a tool connected with the Goddess through womb symbolism. The prototype of the chalice was a gourd, large shell, or a wooden bowl used to contain the sacred liquids used in the rituals of pre-Christian European Paganism. We find the ritual chalice made of silver in magickal systems as late as the Renaissance period. Silver is sacred to the Moon Goddess, and we therefore employ this material for our chalices. In ancient times, the wand was immersed in a wooden bowl or gourd during rituals. In modern times, the athame is often dipped into a chalice (wood to wood and metal to metal, as like attracts like).

Many ritualists employ a mortar and pestle made of wood for ritual in place of the athame and chalice. The word pestle is derived from the Latin *pistillum*. Pistillum is also the origin of the word "pistil," which indicates the ovule-bearing organ of a flower. In this, we see the connection between that which penetrates and that which is penetrated. The word "mortar" is derived from the Latin *mortarium*, indicating both a bowl and a mixture. The etymology of the word "mortar" points towards a receptacle designed to be penetrated and mixed with other substances. In other words, the mortar and pestle are symbols of the procreative act of regeneration and transmutation.

In some rituals, the chalice holds the ritual wine. In matrifocal times, this was the blood of the Goddess and the blood of the Moon contained within the original gourd or bowl. With the rise of patriarchal power and agrarian society, the blood of the Goddess symbolized by red wine became the blood of the Slain God of the harvest. The Cult of Dionysus is perhaps the best-known example.

Within a spiritual context, the chalice is a vessel of offering and receptivity. Just as we, worshippers of deity, are vessels awaiting the pouring forth of spiritual light, so too is the chalice the vessel of containment and fulfillment. The chalice holds the intimate liquids of ritual celebration, just as we ourselves are filled with red liquid essence. In this concept, we find affinity with the chalice and in the relationship of being filled and emptied in our own existence. The chalice is not so much a tool representative of Elemental Water; the chalice's power lies more in its potential, in what it can hold, rather than in the concept it symbolizes.

The Chalice in Modern Paganism

In the rites of systems like Wicca and related groups, the chalice is often used in a symbolic ritual called the Great Rite. Here, it symbolizes the womb of the Goddess, and in conjunction with the wand or athame, it represents the harmonious union of opposites. In this light, the chalice is often associated with fertility.

The chalice is also used to contain wine for rituals and for making libations to the Earth and the Moon. This involves dipping fingers into the wine, shaking off the liquid upward to the Moon, and then pouring out a portion of wine on the Earth. This act of reverence connects one spiritually to "above" and "below" and serves to return the essence of the ritual back to its power.

In some systems, the chalice is known as the "Witching Cup" and is passed around within a ritual circle. It contains wine or an herbal brew, and each member drinks a portion in a symbolic act of joining together in kinship. The chalice can contain a potion to induce altered states of consciousness, and each participant drinks some of it. This will later culminate in an astral or guided imagery journey.

In modern times, the chalice is used at handfasting or wedding ceremonies. Here it serves as the "loving cup" from which the couple drinks to symbolically join themselves together in an intimate bond.

The Chalice as an Elemental Tool

The chalice is traditionally made of silver, which connects it to the Moon, and is associated with the Element of Water. The Moon is the magickal light of the Otherworld that shines upon a body of water such as an ocean, a lake, a pond, or even a well. To hold the chalice containing a liquid is to symbolically hold the essence of magick.

As a tool associated with Water, the Elemental tonal can be sounded over the chalice to awaken its connections to the life-giving and dissolving properties. As noted earlier, the sound is the letter "o" stretched out with the breath–*Oooooo*. To enhance this, you use the Elemental invoking star, which is traced over the chalice.

One special use of the chalice is to bless, consecrate, imbue, or cleanse with the liquid within it. Objects can be dipped into the chalice, or a portion of its contents can be poured over something you want influenced or affected. Think in terms of what the water represents and what the wine represents. This will help you decide on what you want to accomplish.

Just before using the liquid, you can speak words such as "in the name of..." or "by the power of..." to indicate the source that oversees the process. You should indicate what you are bringing about by using words such as "I bless" or "I consecrate" and then stating the influence or effect desired. Here is an example:

> *"In the name of the Goddess of Moon, I consecrate this object to be in her service."*

Another example:

> *"I imbue this object with the dissolving force of Water and remove all contamination."*

The words are finalized by pouring out the liquid or immersing the object in the chalice.

Consecration of the Chalice

Unlike the other ritual tools, the chalice is not "charged" but is instead blessed, devoted, or consecrated (it does, however, contain charged fluids). Ideally, this should be performed beneath the Full Moon. From a mystical perspective, this is best done when the Moon is in the sign of Pisces, Cancer, or Scorpio. These are all Water signs, the most psychic signs of the Zodiac, and are also connected to anything fluid, whether it's frozen, steam, or liquid.

To begin, place a cup of water, a cup of wine, and your chalice on a work area outside beneath the Moon. If you cannot work outdoors, place your work area near a window or on a balcony from which you can see the Moon. Hold the chalice up to the Moon and say:

"I dedicate this chalice to the Moon,
to the Goddess of the Moon, to the Night,
and to the deep mysteries concealed in the
black depths of the outer space."

Set the chalice down and hold the cup of water up to the Moon and say:

"With this water that represents the mystical
essence of the Moon, I imbue the chalice with this
virtue and character. I pour into the chalice the
timeless primordial waters blessed by the Moon's
light through the ages."

Pour the water into the chalice and then hold the chalice up to the Moon and say:

> *"Chalice, you are the bearer and container of the Moon's mystical essence."*

Next, rock the chalice back and forth to give motion to the water (don't be concerned about spilling). As you do this, say:

> *"You wield the Element of Water."*

Now, pour the water back into the cup and then hold the cup of wine up to the Moon and say:

> *"With this wine that represents the sacred life blood of the Mysteries, I imbue the chalice with the Magick of Birth, Life, Death, and Rebirth."*

Pour the wine into the chalice, hold the chalice up to the Moon, and say:

> *"Chalice, you contain the wine of sacrament, the sacred life blood of the Mysteries of Birth, Life, Death, and Rebirth."*

At this stage, if desired, you can verbally dedicate the chalice to the service of a particular goddess.

Now, pour the wine back into the cup. Leave the chalice on your work area and take the cup of water and wine to an area outside where you can toss the liquids up towards the Moon. Once you have done this, return to the work area. Clean the cups and the chalice and put them away.

Chapter Five Test

1. What natural objects were used in olden days that came before the chalice?

2. What other ritual or magickal vessel shares the nature and character of the chalice?

3. What does the chalice represent in the Great Rite?

4. What is one of the purposes of the Witching Cup?

5. In connection with the "sacred life blood," what are the four mysteries imbued into the chalice?

6. What is the purpose of offering libations from the chalice?

7. How can the water or wine in a chalice be applied?

Chapter Six

The Ritual Circle and Its Casting

In this chapter, we will explore various aspects that connect with and empower the concept of a ritual or magickal circle. A circle is a demarcation that sets one space from another. It is also a sacred or magickal zone secured within a specific area. In addition, the circle is a barrier that contains inside and protects against anything entering from outside if it.

As we will see in this chapter, the construction of the circle uses the Four Elements of Creation. In this way, it mimics the ancient myth that Creation came about through the unification of the Air, Fire, Water, and Earth (directed by Spirit). In this light, the casting of a circle is the creation of a mini-universe or microcosm by the ritualist who serves as Spirit in the process of Creation.

The four tools (wand, athame, chalice, and pentacle) are the physical means of connecting with the Four Elements on the Material Plane. Such a connection places the Elemental Forces almost literally in the hands of the ritualist. In other words, the material tools are the counterparts of the Elemental Forces, which allows the ritualist to wield them in the Material Dimension.

Sacred Space

Since ancient times, people have designated or marked-off specific areas as sacred. This served to help people experience something unique and unattached to mundane life. Originally, people discovered areas that emanated a special quality or were led to them by something outside of the mortal realm. Over time, humans began building temples and other structures and held them to be sacred gathering sites.

In modern times, a ritual circle is often referred to "sacred space" and while it certainly can be, ritual circles most often call for activity. Sacred space, in its purest concept, is about being. It is about the stillness that allows spiritual communication to freely flow undistracted and unhampered. In this light, sacred space is more in line with a temple-setting.

From another perspective, sacred space can be a state of consciousness attained through methods like meditation. In this way, a person can enter a sphere of energy that encloses them. Here, the individual is self-contained and is not reliant upon any constructed building or formal ritual circle. Therefore, a person can connect with sacred space within a meadow, high on a mountain top, and so on.

Ritual Space

The performance of ritual is very often associated with the creation of a circle marked upon the ground or floor. It is traditionally large enough for an altar to be set in the center, and with enough room for the ritualist to move around inside the circle. Ritual circles are often constructed with the idea of containment of the energy raised within it as well as establishing an impenetrable barrier. For such purposes, the ritual circle is envisioned as a sphere that surrounds the ritualist—overhead, beneath, and around.

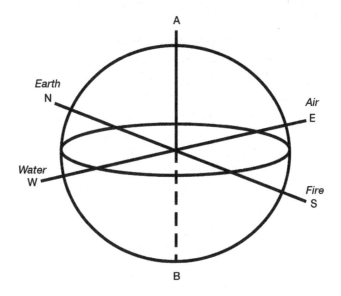

This is sometimes referred to as "the world between the worlds" because the cast circle is believed to exist outside the Material Realm and the non-Material Realm. The perimeter of the circle touches upon what are known as the Elemental Gateways. They occupy the points known as the Four Quarters: North, East, South, and West. These in turn connect with the Four Elements: Earth, Air, Fire, and Water.

Center

Every ritual circle has a center. This area is where energy gathers and is focused before being made available to the direction of the ritualist. It is for this reason that the altar traditionally occupies the center space of the ritual or magickal circle.

The directional quarters of the circle, which are also the Elemental quarters, surround the center at equal intervals.

Imaginary lines drawn into the circle from each quarter creates a four-way intersection, an equilateral cross. The intersection is the center of the circle. The altar is placed there in such a position that the center of the intersecting lines marks the direct center of the altar.

In essence, all movement within the circle revolves around the altar. It is the sacred and magickal center of the circle. All clockwise movement enhances the building of energy, while counterclockwise movement dissolves accumulated energy. This is the "waxing" and "waning" operation of the ritual circle.

Portals

One of the mystical concepts of the ritual circle is that it interfaces with access points into the Elemental Plane. In some traditions, these gateways are protected by Guardians. In some modern systems, these Beings are Elemental Kings or Rulers. In other systems, they are celestial or even chthonic beings. This ties in with the idea of the Great Watchers, the Lords of the Watchtowers.

In occult philosophy, a corridor is envisioned between the physical dimension and Elemental Realm (or what is sometimes called the Plane of Forces). Metaphysical gateways exist between these two planes of existence. They can be opened through rituals and magickal techniques.

Once a portal is open, beings from the Elemental Realm can cross directly into the ritual space. It is important to have an environment in which the Elementals spirit can function. Because the Elementals are etheric beings of Earth, Air, Fire, and Water, their physical counterparts need to be present. It is for this reason that the altar is set with a burning candle (Fire), smoking incense (Air), a chalice (Water), and a container of salt or sand (Earth).

The Elementals will anchor to the physical representations of the Four Elements. This allows them to operate in the ritual environment. It is not unlike a human requiring an oxygen tank to explore the depths of a large body of water.

Barriers & Protection

Creating a ritual circle involves establishing a barrier of protection for the ritualist. This is often necessary because once portals between the worlds are open, it is possible for unwanted entities to cross in the circle. To avoid this, the energy field of the circle needs to be charged.

Charging the circle involves sending a specific frequency of energy into it. The vibration of the energy is contrary to that of undesired entities, and they are in effect repelled by the force field. Specific incantations, scent, symbolism, and ritual tools are used in time-proven ways to ensure that the ritual circle is safe and secure. This also includes applying energy to the gateways or portals at the North, East, South, and West quarters of the marked-out ritual space.

Once a ritual circle is fully cast, the ritualist should not step in and out of circle. In other words, the edge of the circle should be treated like a wall. A doorway is needed for passage. One occult teaching is the ritualist's astral body can be injured if they walk through the unopened energy field of the circle. The perimeter of the circle therefore needs to be opened to allow safe passage to and from. While the circle is open, a blade or a broom is placed in the opening to prevent anything unwanted from entering.

Casting a Ritual Circle

Before casting the circle, read through this chapter's material. You will find material that explains and enhances the casting process. For now, read through the ritual setup and try to envision yourself doing each step. Familiarize yourself with the procedures and movements. Then, move on and read the material following afterwards. That material will provide a deeper understanding of your role in casting a circle. Once this is done, you can then perform the circle casting as given here.

Needed Items for Circle Casting

- 4 white Quarter candles
- 2 white altar candles
- 6 candle holders
- 1 object to serve as altar (set in center of circle)
- 1 black altar cloth (large enough to fully cover altar)
- 1 God and Goddess statue or symbolic representations
- 4 Elemental bowls (filled with associated material unique to each Element)
- 1 incense burner (a censer with chain is preferred)

- 1 silver bell
- Ritual tools: athame, wand, chalice, pentacle

Mark out your circle, making sure it is large enough for you and an altar (with space to walk around it). Place four candle holders with candles, one to each quarter of the circle, and set your altar as follows:

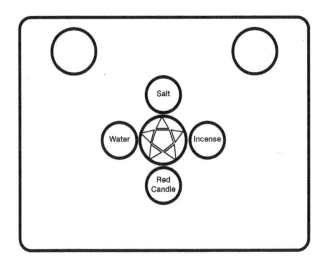

Lay a black altar cloth over the altar. In the center, place the pentacle and surround it with bowls containing representations of the Four Elements. Above the pentacle is Earth, to the right is Air, on the bottom is Fire, and to the left is Water. Place a candle in the back area as shown by the two circles. The area on the left is the Goddess area and on the right is the God area. The altar pictured above faces North.

The placement of the ritual tools is as follows: wand next to the incense bowl, athame beneath the red candle bowl, and the chalice to the left of the water bowl. Set an altar bell next to the wand. If you want to set other things on the altar, think in terms of their Elemental nature and then set them in that general area.

Conjure the Elementals by ringing the bell over each Elemental bowl thrice, beginning North, moving to each one clockwise, and reciting:

> *"I call out into the mist of Hidden Realms and conjure you, spirits of Earth and Air and Fire and Water. Gather now at this sacred circle and grant me union with your powers."*

Ring altar bell over Elemental bowls again thrice and then tap each bowl thrice with the athame. Next, sound out the tonal for each of the Elements (directing your voice to each corresponding bowl):

Earth: *Aaaaaaa*
Air: *Eeeeeeeee*
Fire: *Iiiiiiiiiii*
Water: *Oooooo*

Place the tip of the athame over the Earth bowl and move it around over all the bowls in a clockwise motion. Do this three times as it will stir the Elements into an active state.

After this, raise the athame upward in a manner that symbolizes drawing the Elemental Forces.

Beginning North, tread around the circle while pointing the tip of the athame down along its perimeter. As you do so, speak these words:

> *"By the Forces and Nature of the Four Elements,*
> *I conjure this circle of power;*
> *become a barrier and protection,*
> *a sphere that will serve to contain*
> *the power raised within.*
> *Such is the charge made here"*

Beginning East, and returning there, light each quarter candle, saying:

> **East:** *"Element of Air, I set you here,*
> *fixed to this Circle. Lend your power."*
> **South:** *"Element of Fire, I set you here,*
> *fixed to this Circle. Lend your power."*
> **West:** *"Element of Water, I set you here,*
> *fixed to this Circle. Lend your power."*
> **North:** *"Element of Earth, I set you here,*
> *fixed to this Circle. Lend your power."*

Finish by walking around the circle, athame pointed down, as you sound out the Elemental tonals, all strung together in one long sound:

> *"Eeeeeee-Iiiiiii-Ooooooo-Aaaaaaaaaa"*

Conjuration of the Guardians

At the altar, say the invocation:

> *"I call to You, O' Ancient Ones!*
> *You who dwell beyond the Realms,*
> *You who once reigned in the Time before Time.*
> *Come! Hear the Call!*
> *Assist me to open the Way between the Worlds!"*

Take the pair of altar candles to the East quarter and set them on the ground in front of you. Go to the altar and bring your wand back to the East quarter. Use it to trace a five-pointed star in the air, while saying:

> *"I evoke the presence of the*
> *Guardian of the East."*

Next, place the wand on the ground and pick up to two candles in holders. Bring them together so they touch. Then pause for a moment, extend them out in front of you, and slowly pull them away from each other (as though opening a set of drapes). As you do so, say:

> *"Open the Gateway, grant me*
> *access to the Inner Planes."*

Repeat this procedure at each of the four quarters, giving the appropriate quarter name (East, South, West, North).

Return to the altar with the candles, set them in place, and then retrieve the wand. Hold the wand in your right hand, tap the bottom end firmly on the altar three times, and say:

"I declare this circle to be properly cast!"

Dissolving a Cast Circle

Beginning at the North quarter and then counterclockwise to each quarter, give ritual salute and recite:

"Hear me, Old Ones,
I give thanks for Your attendance
and bid You now depart to your secret Realms.
May there always be peace between us,
may you always look with favor upon me."

(Quarter candle is put out with reverence before moving on to the next quarter.)

Repeat the above action at each of the quarters (moving West, South, East and North again).

Return to altar and pick up your athame. Point blade down towards circle and tread the same direction as above. As you move along, sense the energy being drawn from the circle into your athame. Once the circle has been tread, put the tip of the blade on the pentacle on the altar. Tap it three times to release the energy into the pentacle. This will ground it.

Extinguish all other ritual flames. The circle is dissolved.

Opening a Doorway to and from the Circle

Because a properly cast circle is sealed within an energy sphere, the perimeter must be opened if someone leaves or enters it. Afterwards, it needs to be resealed. There are a couple of methods for this purpose. The usual ritual items are the athame, wand, and broom.

To open a circle, lay the wand and athame together (and touching) on the floor (with tips forward) inserted into the edge of the circle. Picture this as half of each tool is inside the circle, and the other half is outside. Next, pull each tool away as far as your arms will extend out to the sides.

Visualize a double curtain in front of you. Place palms together and insert them between the curtains. Separate your hands and visualize you are parting the curtains wide enough to pass through the opening.

When you are ready to step through, take a broom with you and place it sideways across the opening of the circle. This will act as a temporary barrier.

When you are ready to return, pick up the broom and walk in the circle. Immediately set it down in front of the opening. Next, spread your arms out to the envisioned ends of the curtains and pull them closed. Then, slide the wand and athame back together in the center of the circle opening. Once they meet, quickly pull them back into the circle. This will reseal the energy and secure your circle.

To affirm, tap the end of the athame on the ground, three times and say:

"The circle is sealed and sound again."

Mastery Within the Circle

When casting a circle, remember that you are creating a microcosm, a mini-universe over which you preside. In this realm, you are master and command the Four Elements. Therefore, when working inside the circle, take on a magickal persona (an image of you in a higher nature). This is not unlike the mindset of a child pretending to be a superhero and mimicking that character in movement and voice.

Once the persona is in place, begin to set the altar. Take a black cloth and shake it in the air, allowing it to float down on to the altar guided by your hands. Envision this as the fabric of magick, the blackness of procreation from which all things are generated. Once the cloth is on the altar, smooth and adjust it so it evenly covers the top surface.

Set the pentacle directly on the center of the altar. Envision that you are setting the essence of manifestation in motion. This is the point at which you will direct all otherworldly forces into the Material Dimension. In keeping with this theme, surround the pentacle with four bowls, each containing a representation of an Element. This arrangement was provided in an earlier chapter.

Once in place, the lighting of candles follows. It symbolizes the presence of the Divine, which brings the Four Elements into harmony. In this light, the Elements work together (under direction) to bring about and maintain manifestation during the ritual. Begin by placing a single candle on the altar before you. Focus your thoughts on it as a representation of the presence of the Divine, unlimited by human concepts and imagery. Light the candle. Here, it emanates into the black space, illuminating the Four Elements in the outward center.

Place two candles at the back of the altar, separated, and set them off to the left and right. Take a match and light it from the center candle. Envision the "undefined" essence of divinity separating itself into feminine and masculine polarity. Move the lighted match to the left candle and envision this as the presence of the divine feminine. Next, light the candle to the right, and envision this as the divine masculine. In doing so, you establish the female and male polarities in the process of fertile creativity.

Connect with the presence of "triad divinity" by picking up your wand and tracing a triangle with it from the center flame to the left flame, to the right flame, and then back again. This joins you with the principle and joins the components of the principle with each other.

To connect all of this to the Four Elements, or more correctly to their representations, use the wand to trace a triangle over each of the Elemental bowls in this order: Air, Fire, Water, and Earth. Envision that the essence of divine energy passes from the wand to the items in the bowls. To call the Element into the bowl, ring the bell over each (as prescribed in the ritual) and envision a spiral emerging and floating on the surface of the bowl.

To gather this energy, envision each spiral rising and then resting over the pentacle. They all join into one larger spiral. Use the point of the athame to "hook" the spiral, which you can then lift off the pentacle. The spiraling energy surrounding your athame is Elemental Power that you now wield in your hands.

While casting the circle with the athame, envision that the Elemental energy flowing off your athame and pouring across the perimeter of the circle as you walk along. Envision this as a blue light that forms the edge of the circle. At the completion of this phase, you have created, and you command, a mini-universe in which to perform rituals and magick.

Tips for Ritual Circle Work

- Use a rope, stones, or other objects to mark out and define the circle area
- Place the altar exactly in the center of the circle
- Place the pentacle on the exact center of the altar
- Use Elemental pentagrams to enhance the ritual power
- Move clockwise within a circle
- When dissolving the circle, move counterclockwise
- Maintain ritual space by keeping candles lit and incense burning
- If wearing a robe, watch out so that the sleeves don't meet candle flames
- Don't let mishaps cause you to abandon your ritual or work in a circle
- After any ritual, eat and drink something to ground

Appendix A: Test Answers

Chapter One

1. What is the name of the ancient Greek credited with creating a cohesive teaching of the Four Elements?
    Empedocles.

2. What is the Fifth Element?
    Spirit.

3. What is the dominant force of Earth?
    Dry.

4. What is the dominant force of Air?
    Moist.

5. What is the dominant force of Fire?
    Warm.

6. What is the dominant force of Water?
    Cool.

7. In the context of this chapter, what does the pentagram represent?
   The power of the Four Elements held in balance and harmony by the Fifth Element.

8. What is the magickal nature of Earth?
   Cohesive.

9. What is the magickal nature of Air?
   Transmission.

10. What is the magickal nature of Fire?
    Transformation.

11. What is the magickal nature of Water?
    Movement.

12. What is another title for the Elemental Plane?
    The Plane of Forces.

13. What is the tonal sound associated with the following Elements:
    Earth: Aaaaaa
    Air: Eeeee
    Fire: Iiiii
    Water: Ooooo

14. What Beings are associated with each of the Four Elements?
    Earth: Gnomes
    Air: Sylphs
    Fire: Salamanders
    Water: Undines

Chapter Two

1. What materials are pentacles made of traditionally?
   Clay or metal

2. What is one use of the pentacle at a ritual Quarter?
   To open or close a portal to the Otherworld.

3. What is the purpose of marking additional symbols besides the five-pointed star on the pentacle?
   To link the sacred or mystical Elements of the practitioner to the Material Plane; this connects material and non-material reality.

4. Which device of the Spiritual Warrior is represented by the pentacle?
   The shield.

5. What does the five-pointed star on the pentacle represent?
   The Four Elements of Earth, Air, Fire, and Water held in harmony through the presence of Divine Spirit.

6. What is the Tonal Sound for each of the Four Elements?
   Earth: A
   Air: E
   Fire: I
   Water: O

7. How does the pentacle draw or attract the Element of Earth?
   Through the principle of "like attracts like" and through the magickal charge given to it in preparing the tool.

8. Why can the pentacle be considered the Center of Operation within a ritual or magickal circle?
   Because through it the Four Elements can be evoked or invoked, and this allows the creation of the ritual circle and aids the magick raised within it.

9. What is intended by carrying the pentacle around the area where the ritual or magickal circle is to be set?
   This announces that the circle is to be set in accord with the force of Earth and will hold the properties of protection and containment.

10. What does the "Elemental Star" on the pentacle symbolize in addition to reflecting the Four Elements?
    It represents the concept that we can interface with the Elements and work with them through the nature of the pentacle.

Chapter Three

1. What is one of the earliest trees from which wands were made?
   Beech.

2. What were trees worshipped in ancient times?
   Because it was believed they were inhabited by deities and spirits.

3. What was the significance of carrying a staff from the Sacred Grove in ancient tradition?
   It represented the training and devotion of a priest or priestess.

4. What does the body measure from the inside of the elbow to the tip of the index represent in the wand's length?
   The ability and willingness of the priestess or priest to extend themselves to the greater community.

5. Why is the wand associated with Elemental Air?
   Because it was once a tree branch moved by the wind.

6. Why is the wand associated with Elemental Fire?
   Because ancient people believed that fire resided inside wood.

7. How is the wand held to open and to close portals?
   To open a portal, the wand is held vertical, and to close one, it is held horizontal.

8. What does the wand represent when placed within a chalice?
   The fertility transmitter and the "divine" phallus.

9. How is the wand used to announce the beginning or ending of something in a ritual setting?
   The base is tapped upon the altar three times after words of declaration are spoken.

10. What is the key idea behind the wand in magickal use?
    It is directional in its concept and connected with Elemental forces that evoke and invoke.

Chapter Four

1. What does the double-edged blade of the athame symbolize?
   It symbolizes that the athame operates within material reality as well as within non-material reality.

2. What does the black handle on the athame symbolize?
   The state of procreation from which all things issue forth.

3. What nature does the Element of Air bring to the athame?
   Personal will, discernment, and mental focus.

4. What does the Element of Fire bring to the athame?
   Transformation, power, and force.

5. What is the athame never used for?
   Cutting, carving or any mundane purpose.

6. What does the use of a lodestone pass to the athame?
   It magnetizes and therefore adds the ability of the athame to attract.

7. How is the athame used in the presence of a doorway or portal?
   It is used to invoke protection or to block access. This is accomplished by tracing the five-pointed star.

8. How is the athame used to open and close the ritual circle?
   It can cut an opening in the perimeter of the circle. Removing the athame allows the circle to reseal.

Chapter Five

1. What natural objects were used in olden days that came before the chalice?
   Shell, gourds, and carved wooden bowls.

2. What other ritual or magickal vessel shares the nature and character of the chalice?
   The cauldron.

3. What does the chalice represent in the Great Rite?
   The womb of the Goddess or the womb of the Earth.

4. What is one of the purposes of the Witching Cup?
    To join a group of people in declared kinship.

5. What are the four mysteries imbued into the "sacred life blood" of the chalice?
    Birth, life, death, and rebirth.

6. What is the purpose of offerings and libations from the chalice?
    To honor the Moon and the Underworld, that which is above and below.

7. How can the water or wine in a chalice be applied?
    The liquid can be used to anoint an object as the desired effect is spoken. It can also bless, consecrate, imbue, or dissolve impurities.